Carol Grace
Rider

Some Angels Have Four Paws

Life Lessons From Our Dogs

Carol Grace Anderson, M.A.

Rock Hill Publishing
Nashville

Rock Hill Publishing
PO Box 148258
Nashville, TN 37214-8258
Toll-free: 877-446-9364
Fax: 615-885-2466
E-mail: RockHillBooks@aol.com
www.SomeAngels.com

Book design: Gena Kennedy

Photography: Back Photo by Dan Helland
All other photos by Carol Grace Anderson

Printed in the United States of America

ISBN: 0-9660276-1-2

*This book is dedicated to
my entire loving family. You've
always had a huge heart for
animals. That started it all.*

*It's also dedicated to you
wonderful pet lovers reading
this book. You may have learned
more lessons than you realize
from a special dog in your life.*

Also by Carol Grace Anderson ...
Get Fired Up Without Burning Out!
& Get Fired Up! (10 Song CD)

Why this book?

I barely squeaked through high school. To make matters worse, I went on to flunk out of three colleges.

Finally, I buckled down to reach my goals—which required a college degree. After earning a B.A. in Psychology and a Masters in Counselor Education, I realized that formal education isn't such a bad thing.

Truthfully, however, I've learned more life lessons from my dog, Cowgirl, than from any college course. My precious friend also taught me a lot about loss.

This book is about reminding you of those powerful lessons and maybe in sharing in the healing process if you've lost your beloved pet.

Enjoy this short and sweet journey with me, and please feel free to share your journey by posting your comments and stories on our web site, www.SomeAngels.com.

Contents

Part One

Part Two: Lessons

Part Three

Part One:

Meeting

*All the knowledge, the totality
of all questions and answers,
is contained in the dog.*

Franz Kafka

On that cold and rainy Friday afternoon, we stood at the front door saying goodbye. After a vigorous workout at the gym and a lovely lunch, my sister Mary Beth, our friend Lisa, and I were going our separate ways—starting our weekend.

That's when we saw him slowly walking by, casually looking over at us now and then. We couldn't help but notice that longish blond hair blowing in the cold wind ... partly covering big, warm, brown eyes. Kind of a cowboy type.

I said, "Hey, come here a minute." He pretended he didn't hear me and looked the other way. "C'mon over here, Cowboy," I insisted.

Finally, he looked around and slowly sauntered over toward the door. "How cute!" we all said in unison. But he looked like he'd spent a year out in the rain, the woods, the mud ... you name it.

Somehow, the three of us could see way beyond the dirt to something kind of special. Maybe he'd like a drink, we thought.

He treated every sip of that water like it was fine champagne. The bowl was nearly empty when I offered him a cold hot dog (the only thing in the fridge). We all stood on the front step watching as he slowly savored each bite of it.

*No matter how little money
and how few possessions you own,
having a dog makes you rich.*

Louis Sabin

It seemed as though I had seen this Benji look-alike in the neighborhood before. Always looked kind of lost, as I recall.

We all said our good-byes ... again ... to each other and to "Cowboy".

The quietness in my cozy, new condo was deafening.

At the time, I was part of the Roy Clark show, and would usually be on the road ... especially on a Friday. It was fun to travel all over the country singing in large concert halls, fairs, and even doing the Tonight Show. But after years of constant travel, I learned that there really IS no place like home ... even for just a few days.

Unpacking boxes became too tedious for a weekend off, so I started surfing the TV channels. Realizing that I left my glasses in the car, I ran out in the rain ... only to see "Cowboy" sitting there.

"Didn't you go home yet?" I wondered. He seemed to be patiently guarding my small driveway ... protecting me from I don't know what.

After a big bag of microwave popcorn and nothing much on the tube, I opened the front door slightly to see if he was still around. Big as life,

*The bond with a true dog
is as lasting as the ties
of this earth will ever be.*

Konrad Lorenz

there he was … looking up at me with almost a sweet smile.

What in the world should I do? Call the humane shelter? The dog pound? Or just forget about it altogether?

Of course, forgetting about him was not an option. But I had a dilemma. I hated to see this neat dog sitting out in the now-freezing rain, but I had off-white carpet in my new place. Muddy paw prints wouldn't add much to the look I was going for.

Also, I thought that maybe his owner might be searching for him. I wondered if he belonged to a family, if he was wild, if he needed shots—every-thing was running through my head.

What to do? I spread an old sheet on the living room rug and went outside to have a heart-to-heart talk with this guy:

> *"If you will promise to stay on a sheet all night, until the morning when I can find your family or have us visit a vet and dog-groomer … you can come in here out of the cold rain. Now, I travel a bunch and don't know what in the world I'd do with you when I leave, but*

Heaven goes by favour. If it went by merit, you would stay out and your dog would go in.

Mark Twain

I'm willing to try to figure some-thing out. Can you work with me on this, Cowboy?"

He looked at me with such understanding eyes, it was clear that he got the whole picture. After my reassuring invitations—about three of them—he stepped through the door and sat smack down in the middle of the old sheet.

I pretty much told him my life history ... the whole enchilada. He was very attentive. After midnight, I explained that I'd be going upstairs to bed and he must stay downstairs on the sheet all night.

At about seven the next morning, I tiptoed down to the living room and there he was ... comfort-ably lying down in the same place. When I opened the door for him to take an outside break he looked up with a grateful look ... thankful for all my hospitality.

Twenty minutes later, there he was again ... right outside, guarding the front door with confidence.

I called all the shelters only to hear that no one had reported a missing dog that fit his description. After another cold hot dog and some water we vis-ited the local animal doctor.

The average dog…
is a nicer person than
the average person.

Andy Rooney

Dr. Evanston said, "She seems like a very healthy, two or three year old, forty pound, sheepdog mix. We'll give her preventive shots and clean her up."

SHE???? Oh, I guess her name will be COWGIRL.

I picked her up that afternoon with her beautiful blond coat shiny and untangled. Now you could clearly see those big, warm, eyes.

She seemed to enjoy inspecting the bag of goodies I returned with: a collar, leash, bowls, special dog food that boasts the most vitamins (do dogs really need vitamins?), and a doggy chew. She knew I was in it for the long haul.

Little did I know, Cowgirl would change my life.

And I'll bet you had no idea how much your beloved pet would influence *your* life.

Part Two:

Lessons

*A great dog is nothing less
than a gift from God.*

CGA

Lesson One: Flexibility

Cowgirl taught me to be flexible. I didn't know how I would manage with on-the-job travel and the new responsibility of this living creature. It felt like an awesome and scary task. Never having kids or a pet of my own, was I up to the challenge? When would I know?

Haven't we all noticed that change is inevitable (except from vending machines)? And change is constant, too. We might as well get used to it. We don't like it much because it's uncomfortable. But we can be resilient creatures … life eases up when we learn how to be more flexible.

Things are changing faster than at any time in history. Now is the time to embrace that change.

Dogs are amazingly flexible. Notice how they adjust to our schedules? Our lifestyles? Our changing circumstances? They don't whine. They don't fret or panic. They just get on with it.

Years ago, Cowgirl and I experienced a level-3 tornado, first-hand. Yikes, what a scary event!

If you think change is stressful...
try not changing.
That's really stressful!

Unknown

When we emerged from the basement, I saw that the backyard looked like a war-zone. Roofing and gutters hung in large, ominous pieces. Trees— huge hundred-year-old trees—were scattered everywhere like pick-up sticks. Telephone poles, with their live wires dangling, lay in splintered piles.

The amazing thing is that the flowers, even the younger, more delicate ones, remained intact— not only because they were closer to the ground, but they were more flexible in the wind!

Through the years, I was forced to be flexible— thanks to Cowgirl. I found kennels, neighbors looking for part-time work, professional pet-sitters, even friends, to care for her when I was on the road.

Although she would prefer to hang out with me, Cowgirl taught me to look for alternatives. When you need 'em, you find 'em.

We really can't control all our circumstances and challenges. We can control our decisions, actions and reactions. That's very powerful when you think about it.

If we were only half as resilient as our dogs, our lives would be lots easier. Their flexibility is awe-

*If we choose to bend with
the ebb and flow of life …
we'll have more joy and peace.*

EGA

some. Just think of how easy and natural it is for dogs to bounce right back after we've had to reprimand them. It's as though they're thinking, *"Okay, that's over, now we're great friends again. Let's romp."*

Walking the dog down a new, unfamiliar path is similar. *"Oh, we're going this way today. How cool."* Or, *"You brought home a new kind of treat. This is fantastic."* Or, *"I guess you have to do some work now. I'll take a nap and try for some attention a little later."* Of course they don't forget to give it another shot soon.

Things happen all day long in our lives that are beyond our control. Let's be more flexible like our dogs are. It works way better.

Whatever you can do, or dream you can, begin it. Boldness has genius, power and magic in it.

Goethe

Lesson Two: Confidence

Cowgirl would take on a mixed pack of wolves, coyotes, and tigers if given the opportunity, truly believing in victory. That's confidence!

We humans have learned to live in fear. We're born with very few innate fears—most experts describe those as fear of falling and fear of loud noise. All other fears are learned, starting at a very young age.

The good news is that, of course, we can unlearn those fears and live more confidently. We just have to do something different to get a different result. The only way is to begin to take more confident actions today. Starting a little at a time, new behaviors spark more new behaviors. It's a process.

Sure, we all need some fear to be safe. We don't want to jump into an empty swimming pool, fall out of a tree, drive without seatbelts. We do want to jump out of our comfort zone and take healthy risks to live more confidently.

Remember when you started driving? It may have

Life is either a daring adventure or nothing.

Helen Keller

seemed kind of risky and confusing, thinking of so many things at once. Now, it's no big deal. It's familiar. It comes naturally.

By taking small new steps consistently, we can overcome our fears in a similar way. Feel the fear and take those new actions. In time, they'll become safe and familiar. We just have to do them. Now.

When it comes to living fearlessly and confidently, Cowgirl wrote the book. She would approach every new person and experience with interest and curiosity. No fear. No judgment.

Her example helped me be more brave and confident.

Dogs are not wimps. Let's follow their lead.

We cherish our friends not
for their ability to amuse us,
but for ours to amuse them.

Evelyn Waugh

Lesson Three: Laughter

Yeah, yeah, they say laughter is the best medicine. You know what? Sure, they're right! (Whoever "they" are.)

I've learned to laugh more from Cowgirl. It's easy for me to take everything way more seriously than necessary. She'd always jump right in there to remind me to "*Lighten up, already.*" When I stop to think about it, I chuckle. She's right!

Isn't it interesting that, in time, we can find something funny about even the most terrible circumstances? Think of the funniest vacation stories. They're about how wrong things went—am I right?

We don't usually remember the smooth, expected, lovely moments. But we never forget the crazy, unpredictable experiences. They were usually the most fun!

On a Saturday afternoon, I was walking with Cowgirl in a field near a church. There was a lot of interesting activity near the open front door of the church. She went over to check things out.

He deserves Paradise who makes his companions laugh.

The Koran

Before I knew what was happening, Cowgirl walked right in and started following the bride! By the time I could get to her (I didn't want to yell), she was halfway down the aisle ... tail wagging all the way. Apparently, she thought everyone was gathered to celebrate her!

When we walked outside, she looked up at me with a *"So, what's the big deal?"* look. I was so embarrassed, but what was there to do but have a good, hearty laugh? In time, it would be a fun story for the bridal couple ... I hope.

Dogs don't get ulcers! When we're caught up in the stressed-out details of life, our pets remind us to chill out. Notice how they know the exact times to step in? They're funny without even trying to be ... without saying one word!

If we can just allow ourselves to be more comfortable with being silly sometimes, we'll get big benefits.

A dog wags its tail
with its heart.

Martin Buxbaum

Lesson Four: Exercise

Exercise? Never liked it much at all. I didn't think I needed it since I always felt pretty good. I've heard others sing the praises of fitness, but wondered why people would spend so much valuable time at it.

Now I've got a frightening new deal to contend with. Dogs need regular exercise … and that means every single day … Cowgirl included. I learned that if you don't have a fenced-in yard, then at least short daily walks are essential.

This was a rude awakening to my leisurely morning routine of coffee and the newspaper in my bathrobe. It changed to get up, get dressed, and get out a-walkin'.

Some beautiful stuff happened. Cowgirl led me to enjoy new, wonderful experiences.

I never realized how enchanting a walk in light rain could be. It was mysterious, energizing and a good facial moisturizer to boot!

Keep that oxygen comin'
the heart pumpin'
the blood flowin'
the attitude zoomin'.

EGcA

The spring burst into yellow and purple wildflowers that I had never seen. If it weren't for Cowgirl, I wouldn't have experienced the fragrance of those lilacs and sweet honeysuckle framing the woods where we walked.

Summer mornings were alive with clusters of kids on their bikes, all excited about their break from school. We got to know some of them and watched them grow up ... so fast.

Autumn was loaded with brilliant color, smells of burning leaves, and blaring sounds of the high-school band practicing on the field for their half-time show. It took me right back to majorette practice for our football half-time shows so long ago.

Cold, bitter, winter nights were another story. Cowgirl relished every moment of it. I dreaded it. The freezing mornings, though, were somehow exhilarating. That clear, cold air was a powerful wake-up to start the day.

Snow is always fun, especially in Tennessee where it's a luxury. Once we had a freak storm of seven or eight inches of snow. Cowgirl couldn't get enough of jumping and playing in it ... until she was caked with snow.

I would never have realized the value of regular

*Daily walking is one of
the very best exercises
for just about everyone.*

Medical experts

walking if it weren't for Cowgirl. It has helped me physically, spiritually, and emotionally. I've learned from the experts that getting our blood pumping helps all our organs get more oxygen and work more efficiently.

Since walking is such a plus, I've included aerobics and yoga now and then. They all have benefits. I've added a lot of energy … and maybe years … to my life.

Thanks, Cowgirl, for the hundreds of miles.

Failure is fantastic! It's a step closer to success. It's proof that we're taking action.

CGA

Lesson Five: The Present

Now is really all there is. This very moment. Yesterday's over. Tomorrow isn't here yet. So, here we are … this is it!

Dogs live in the present moment for sure. They're not concerned with last week or last year. They don't seem worried about tomorrow either. They're right here, right now. Whatever they decide to do … they're doin' it.

It's hard for us humans to live that way. Sure, we have many responsibilities and have to plan ahead, but it seems that we fall into the habit of living in the past or the future. We put off the exciting, challenging actions now that will help us realize our dreams.

Why do we put off those important actions? It's that four-letter word again … fear. It keeps us stuck.

Cowgirl has taught me by her example that I need to be more present. Be more mindful of making things happen now. She has shown me that failure is just fine. I've seen her try over and over again to

Far better it is to dare mighty things, to win glorious triumphs even though checkered by failure, than to rank with those poor spirits who neither enjoy nor suffer much because they live in a gray twilight that knows neither victory nor defeat.

Theodore Roosevelt

reach for a runaway errant biscuit or chewy bone that went under the couch. She wasn't embarrassed by all her tries … and never gave up … even if it was way beyond her reach and I had to help.

It's easy to get into that dream-busting habit of putting off the action. That's the philosophy of "Some Day I'll Do It." The problem with that is we keep putting things off and "some day" never comes. It slips right on by. Over and over.

Dogs don't have that ongoing fear of failure. They jump right in and go for it now.

Virgil Thompson once said, "Try a thing you haven't tried before three times … once to get over the fear, once to find out how to do it, and a third time to find out whether you like it or not." Overpower fear with action. Fear must be moved through, not turned from.

Dogs live in the moment and take action now!

*The real secret of success
is enthusiasm.*

Walter Chrysler

Lesson Six: Enthusiasm

To our wonderful dogs, every day is a grand, triumphant celebration. What a way to live!

Each time we come in the door we are welcomed as though we've been gone on a month-long safari. Whether we've been gone five minutes or five hours, it doesn't make one bit of difference in the enthusiasm department.

Enthusiasm comes from the Latin "en theos", or one with the energy of the Divine. That's pretty heady stuff but it makes sense ... enthusiasm is that powerful.

Dogs seem to have this glorious trait quite naturally. When they're getting their basic needs met, dogs never seem depressed. Unfortunately, we humans are rarely enthusiastic 24/7. But it's so pleasurable to be filled with hope. Once again we need to use our dogs as role-models.

Cowgirl has taught me that something as simple as the aroma of pasta cooking can bring great joy. It's the hope of the few strands of spaghetti (her favorite food) that may wind up in her bowl. (Of course it does!)

What beauty and light is in the enthusiasm of a dog.

CGA

I've always been intrigued with the enthusiasm of dogs and wondered what might help us humans get in on the action.

My research has shown that one of the greatest builders of enthusiasm is to have an attitude of gratitude. It's easy to get bogged down with negative thinking ... focusing on what we don't have, rather than truly appreciating what we do have.

You've probably heard about those "grateful journals" that became popular a few years back. They really do help to get in a habit of more positive thinking. I've been reminded several times lately that our only option is our attitude!

Most of the experts say that what we focus on expands in our life. If we fill our minds with the news stories of disaster, bloodshed and heartbreak of every sort, around the globe, it has a powerful effect on us. It's too much for anyone to take in and process the world's pain when there's not much we can do about it ... sadly.

Reminding ourselves over and over how much we do have to feel grateful about can do wonders with our attitude.

Through her actions, Cowgirl has taught me that I could be more enthusiastic about every person

Money will buy a pretty good dog, but it won't buy the wag of his tail.

Henry Wheeler Shaw

I meet. After alerting me, loudly, that someone's at the door, she's found that there's a trait that is very likable and interesting in just about everyone: delivery people, car mechanics, plumbers, neighbors, kids in the park, older folks out for a stroll, Girl Scouts selling cookies, you name it.

I'm working on looking at the people I meet with a new Cowgirl-type open-mindedness and enthusiasm. It can be quite amazing.

Dogs greet every morning with a fresh view of hope and happiness. They seem to erase yesterday's inconveniences ... a scary thunderstorm, a walk outside much later than expected, a rabies shot. Instead, there's the tail-wagging enthusiasm that THIS will be the best day ever!

Aren't they something?

'Tis a gift to be simple,
'Tis a gift to be free,
'Tis a gift to come down
Where we ought to be
And when we find ourselves
In the place that's right
'Twill be in the valley
Of love and delight.

Shaker Hymn from the
Nineteenth~Century

Lesson Seven: Simplicity

Have you noticed the buzz these days about living more simply? There are books about it, classes that teach it, even magazines dedicated to the topic … such interest.

Dogs are a prime example of truly living the simple life. When Cowgirl was younger, she couldn't wait until an empty, crumpled up envelope would miss the trash can. She'd be all over it … having great fun dissecting it and shredding it beyond recognition. So much for fancy dog toys. Simple fun instead.

Maybe we've gone so far into the philosophy of "more is better" that the pendulum is swinging back to the older days of simplicity.

There's been this strong, competitive drive to reach the top. The top of what?

Many financially successful people have been interviewed at length. They have, or could afford, more stuff than they can probably ever use. But you've heard them say that their greatest pleasures

Little things …
can mean so much more.

CGA

come from seeing their child's first school play, or having a quiet morning to read, or fishing for hours in a remote river cove, or savoring a bite of warm, homemade apple pie to top off a family meal. Simple stuff.

We've gone over the top with adding complications to our lives with our "more" lifestyles. The more we have, the more we have to insure, fix, store, clean, move around, etc.

Somehow, we've gotten the impression that not only will more material things enhance our lives, but the more we do, the more fulfilling our lives will be.

Technology seduced us with the promise of giving us more time by doing things faster. What really happened was that we now have technology that helps us stay busy all the time!

Cell phones have given us the opportunity to take care of business while driving, dining out, grocery shopping, attending a concert, everywhere. We are now connected. Is this what we want?

Between the cell phones, palm pilots and laptop computers we can be assured that we can work from the beach, the cab, the park, the baseball game, the plane … whew!

Dogs find great joy in the simplest things...they're thrilled it's morning!

CGA

It's hard, if not impossible, to be present in the glory of this moment without some degree of simplicity. Think back to the carefree days when you were a young kid. What was your favorite toy? Chances are pretty good it was fairly simple.

My 5-year old nephew has more toys and electronic gadgets from loving relatives than he could count. His favorite? Simple, old-fashioned Tinker Toys. He loves to create. His imagination takes him further than the bells and whistles of any video games could. The game of Monopoly has probably held its own for so many decades because of its simplicity.

Margaret Young put it very clearly:

> *"Often people attempt to live their lives backwards; they try to have more things, more money, in order to do more of what they want so that they will be happier. The way it actually works is the reverse. You must first be who you really are, then, do what you need to do, in order to have what you want."*

*Happiness is not getting
what you want, but
wanting what you have.*

Various Sources

Dogs are content with the very basics: love, an uncomplicated bowl of food, a bowl of water, countless naps, walks, and a playtime now and then. They give back so much and expect so little.

Ah, the simple life.

To err is human, to forgive … canine

Unknown

Lesson Eight: Forgiveness

Dogs seem to be the most forgiving creatures on earth. What a lesson we can learn here.

To forgive means to be in favor of giving, to grant free pardon. When we forgive another we are also giving to ourselves. It's a mutual gift.

After we forgive, we need to go the next step—to forget. We want to remember the lessons we learned, but we don't want to carry around heavy baggage from the past.

My friends and I met for lunch recently and talked about forgiving ourselves for our perfectionism. We vowed to help each other deal with our imperfections in a forgiving way so we can move forward. Perfectionism gets in the way of everything. We don't have to prove we're okay by seeking perfection.

Forgiving others and ourselves is not always easy. Sometimes it takes years, or might not happen at all, when the pain is too deep. That's when a professional counselor can help the process.

*Forgiveness is the key
to action and freedom.*

Hannah Arendt

It's worth the work.

The book *Course In Miracles* says that "all disease comes from a state of unforgiveness," and that "whenever we are ill, we need to look around and see who it is we need to forgive."

Cowgirl demonstrated the beauty of forgiveness since we met. If I'd accidentally step on her paw while she was napping on the floor, she'd yelp and cry out in pain. Of course, I'd feel awful too. Two minutes later, she'd walk over with her sore paw to lick my hand and to see if I was okay.

Dogs forgive and forget on a regular basis. Note their strong disappointment every time we leave the house without them. They act as though they'll be forever brokenhearted with their pitifully sad look. When we return, all is back to happy tail wags … forgiven and forgotten.

Dear God, I pray for patience.
And I want it right now!

Oren Arnold

Lesson Nine: Patience

Since we were kids we've been told, "Be patient. Wait. It'll be your turn soon." Sound familiar? And how hard was it to be still and wait? We wanted to open those presents now. We wanted to go out and play now. We wanted that ice cream now. Later wasn't an understandable option.

Dogs, along with their wonderful enthusiasm, seem to have an innate capacity to be patient. Cowgirl tried to teach me early on that things will happen when they're supposed to. I wasn't quite ready for that lesson then.

Through the years, I've been confused by the message, "Take action now. Be persistent," at the same time knowing how important it is to relax and be patient.

What I think the real truth is? We need to do both —be content right now and enjoy the journey even as we patiently trudge forward.

If we don't enjoy the process, we probably won't

Patience may be the highest virtue ... but it's so doggone difficult!

CGA

be happy when we arrive. Living in the future—only looking ahead—is the model of impatience. You've heard it many times … "I can't wait till summer" … "I can't wait till I retire" … "I can't wait till Christmas" … "I can't wait to have my desk organized" … fill in the blanks.

Impatience is very stressful. It's fueled by thoughts of "I should" … "What if" … "I have to" … "If only." Those frenzied thoughts rob us of any possibility of enjoying the journey.

Letting go of that old perfection syndrome … feeling that we must do everything perfectly or not at all … is a powerful antidote to impatience. It takes practice and support, but it's worth it. And we learn more from our mistakes than our successes.

Salvador Dali said it plainly: "Have no fear of perfection … you'll never reach it."

The experts agree that the more patient we are with ourselves and our circumstances, the more patient we are with others. That's a nice payoff … and a great relief to the others we've been impatient with.

Years ago, when I took Cowgirl to dog training school, she won the blue ribbon … not for heeling, not for turning, not for overall obedience (not

*No thing great is created
suddenly, any more than a
bunch of grapes or a fig. If
you tell me that you desire
a fig, I answer you that there
must be time. Let it first
blossom, then bear fruit,
then ripen.*

Epictetus
circa 50 - 120 a.d.

this rebel) … but for staying.

When the whole class commanded our dogs to "lie down and stay", even as we walked around, Cowgirl stayed the longest. She was the most patient.

The blue ribbon will always remind me of that day, and to remember to be patient and "stay". Stay in the moment, here and now.

*Man is a dog's idea of
what God's should be.*

Holbrook Jackson

Lesson Ten: Spirituality

The dictionary defines the word spiritual as "pertaining to the spirit or soul as distinguished from the physical nature." So, "spiritual" refers to a higher plane in general—the Light of the world.

Most descriptions of a balanced life include spirituality as a piece of the whole puzzle. Of course there are many different belief systems of what it actually is ... or how to get there.

My feeling is that spirituality is a relationship with God, a Higher Power who is way beyond us mortals—a power we can learn vital information from. After all, God ... the power ... created each one of us ... humans and animals and flowers ... even storms ... all of it.

Much of this book is really about the traits we associate with God: forgiveness, patience, open-mindedness, enthusiasm, love, and so on. Traits we all strive for.

Dogs can be the vehicle to bring us to a deeper

Recollect that the Almighty,
who gave the dog to be
companion of our pleasures
and our toils, hath invested
him with a nature noble...
and incapable of deceit.

Sir Walter Scott

spirituality. This might happen directly by their unwitting example, or indirectly. Or both.

My walks with Cowgirl have opened my eyes, mind, and heart to thoughts and beauty I had never experienced. One freezing cold February morning as we walked in the park, I noticed the frost-covered branches dramatizing every tree. The dancing sun would highlight different sections with sparkling effects.

This wonderland made me want to sing. When I ran out of verses to "He's Got The Whole World In His Hands," I adlibbed: "He's Got You and Me, Cowgirl, In His Hands." She had been walking ahead but stopped short and looked up at me with a look that said, *"Oh yeah, that's true, but sing a little softer!"*

During our hundreds of walks, those times became a spiritual oasis. Often I would talk to God. I'd ask questions, sometimes wondering why things weren't going my way. Mostly, I'd give thanks for the awesome splendor around me ... including Cowgirl.

*Nothing in the world can take
the place of persistence.*

Calvin Coolidge

Lesson Eleven: Persistence

Dogs are persistent. They'll retrieve a ball countless times in a row. They'll go for walks as often as they can. They'll dig up a bone that's been buried forever—all in great spirits.

All success comes from persistence. Imagine the many stumbling blocks in the way of inventors … but they turned those blocks into stepping stones toward success. They persevered.

Now, we can enjoy the fruits of their persistence. New medications and treatments, higher food production, greater diagnostic tools … improvements that have increased our life expectancy by leaps and bounds.

Louis Pasteur wrote, "Let me tell you the secret that has led to my goal. My strength lies solely in my tenacity."

Many successful people didn't reach success on the merits of good grades, talent, or opportunity alone. But by their unyielding persistence, they moved forward.

To his dog, every man is King; hence the constant popularity of dogs.

Aldous Huxley

Jack Canfield and Mark Victor Hansen came up with a brilliant idea ... to collect powerful short stories with a message, put them into a book, and call it *Chicken Soup for the Soul*.

What sounded like a good idea to them was rejected by every major book publisher in the country. Finally, a little-known publisher in Florida shared the same vision and came through. Now the *Chicken Soup* books have become a best-selling series and have sold millions of copies worldwide!

When Cowgirl became arthritic, her joy of life never wavered for a moment. A ride in the car? Sometimes her legs wouldn't be strong enough to jump into the backseat, but she would persevere and finally make it ... with a little boost from me. Success follows persistence.

No one appreciates the very special genius of your conversation as a dog does.

Christopher Morley

Lesson Twelve: Friendship

What is a friend anyway? A buddy? Supporter? Someone fun to hang out with? A good listener? Someone who knows you well … and still likes you? All of the above?

Dogs are dear, true friends. No matter what. They're right there to listen—our silent partners. They don't criticize what we say or do. They watch us grow. We watch them grow. We have a bond.

Friends come in all sizes, ages, shapes, colors, and personality types. We're very close to some friends. Others are casual, pleasant, but intermittent relationships. We need all of them.

Since real friends are honest with us, we can learn a lot if we're willing to listen. Sure, it's not always easy.

There seems to be a different dynamic between our guy friends and girl friends. They both make good friends and offer important insights with differing points of view. It's refreshing to hear it all.

A friend is a gift you give yourself.

Robert Louis Stevenson

Many years ago, a close circle of twelve women friends and I actually formed a club and called it the Ladies In Progress Society (LIPS). We commit to get-togethers on a regular basis.

One event that's set in stone is a holiday sit-down dinner at the same home every year. We each bring one lavish dish and small gifts for everyone. After dessert, we sing around the grand piano—everything from carols to show tunes to original compositions. It's a treasured evening. There's always wild laughter, sometimes tears, often unrepeatable jokes.

Through the ten years that we've had this friendship club, we've been there for each other through it all: loss, marriage, later-than-usual college degrees, adoptions, sickness, divorce, birthdays, bad haircuts, new relationships ...

As the song says, "That's what friends are for." Speaking of songs, Carole King sums it up:

> *"You just call out my name*
> *And you know wherever I am*
> *I'll come running*
> *To see you again*
> *Winter, spring, summer, or fall*
> *All you have to do is call*
> *And I'll be there, yes I will*
> *You've got a friend."*

*When a man's best friend
is his dog ... that dog
has a problem*

Edward Abbey

Cowgirl has taught me that the best way to have a true friend is to be one ... any time of the day or night, and in any season of life.

Isn't your dog's friendship a treasure?

*Old age means realizing
you will never own all
the dogs you wanted to.*

Joe Gores

Lesson Thirteen: Aging

Whose favorite topic is aging? Well, it is as much a part of life as the rising sun. And it sure beats the alternative.

Dogs are mini-models of our lives in lots of ways. We can see in them the aging process far easier than we can see it in ourselves. Since they age faster, we can learn a lot from them about our own aging.

I'll never forget the first time Cowgirl had to give up her attempts to jump up on the bed for a few soothing words and gentle pats before she curled up for the night. Her arthritis had progressed, but she had found new ways to adjust. The wake-up call had been her paw softly tapping my leg to remind me it was exactly 7:00. Now it turned into tapping the side of the bed. It worked just fine.

Watching the aging process can help us be more accepting of it … even if we don't love the concept. It can be a sad and frustrating piece of life. Aging reminds us of the loss of childhood, loss of youth, loss of loved ones, loss of unwrinkled skin,

*Our only option, even in
aging, is our attitude.*

CGA

sometimes the loss of health.

When the veterinarian casually mentioned in a routine checkup that along with arthritis, Cowgirl was losing some hearing and eyesight, I felt a sinking feeling. He said this is typical of aging in dogs, no big deal.

No big deal? I beg your pardon, Doc. How could this strong, beautiful, vibrant creature be losing anything? It took time, but I finally began to accept the painful truth that we start aging the day we're born. I knew I had to feel the pain and move forward a day at a time.

Along with experiencing much more loss as we age, there's some good stuff that comes along with it. On the flip side, we can take advantage of the painful lessons we've learned.

Don't you wish you knew in high school what you know now?

Things for me would have been a lot different with more wisdom in the mix. And my loving parents would have had fewer sleepless nights. But who knew? We learn as we go … and grow.

It's powerful to talk to elderly folks and hear their take on life. Usually their philosophy is profound

Life can be sweeter
as the years go by.

CGA

... yet it can be put in just a few words. It's that simple.

It's fun to hear what those hundred-year-olds have to say on the Today show when asked for their secret of longevity. You often hear "I laugh a lot" ... "I eat a piece of chocolate every day" ... "I forgive and forget" ... "I walk a mile a day" ... "I volunteer at the Children's Hospital" ... "I dance." It's nothing very heavy.

As Bonnie Wilcox once said, "Old dogs, like old shoes, are comfortable. They might be a bit out of shape and a little worn around the edges, but they fit well."

We love our dogs through their aging process. That can help us love, accept, and be patient with others—and ourselves—through our own aging.

Not Carnegie, Vanderbilt, and Astor together could have raised enough money to buy a quarter share in my little dog.

Ernest Thompson Seton

Lesson Fourteen: Love

T his chapter comes later in the book because after writing down all these lessons from Cowgirl, I now realize it's a lot about love.

Love is much more than a nice feeling. It's uncon-ditional positive regard. Giving and receiving love is a basic need ... for all of us. It can be family love, romantic love, love of friends, pets ...

Dogs love us unconditionally. No matter how absent-minded, uptight, busy, messy, cranky, late, or tired we might be, their love for us never fades. Isn't that remarkable?

From Cowgirl's unconditional love, I learned to have more unconditional love for myself. That hasn't been easy. I somehow had the erroneous notion that I had to strive toward perfection to be more lovable.

Messages like those are rampant in our society and come from many sources. Television, movies, magazines—all give us the impression we should look, think, or be a certain way to be lovable.

*I love a dog. He does nothing
for political reasons.*

Will Rogers

Teachers inadvertently might give the same impressions.

My parents are in the ministry, and as a kid I think I heard so many Bible teachings that I innocently compared myself to God's ideal. Of course, anyone would fall short on that one!

We can only love others to the degree that we love ourselves. Think about it. Loving the self is not pride, arrogance, vanity or self-centeredness ... that's fear. Love includes having great respect for ourselves, imperfections and all.

Oscar Wilde said, "To love oneself is the beginning of a lifelong romance." If we don't love ourselves, how could we expect others to love us?

Loving is an ongoing thing. It's a verb. It's dynamic. It's a great teacher. It generates more love.

I'll never forget one bright, windy spring afternoon. Cowgirl and I were walking in a large field that was just beginning to turn green. The air smelled fresh and sweet. It had been a long winter and even though her joint pain was increasing and her eyesight and hearing going fast, Cowgirl ran around with as much gusto as she could muster. She savored every single minute of it.

Love is the discovery of ourselves in others and the delight in the recognition.

Alexander Smith

As she ran toward me with her long blond hair and red bandana blowing in the wind, her loving eyes said, *"Oh, thank you beyond measure!"*

Love is not jealous or resentful. Love is feeling grateful that those you love are enjoying this moment.

Sophocles wrote, "One word frees us of all the weight and pain of life. That word is love."

Cowgirl has increased my capacity to love, and for that I will be eternally grateful.

*Dogs are our link to paradise.
They don't know evil or
jealousy or discontent.*

Milan Kundera

Lesson Fifteen: Loss

Life is full of good-byes. Sometimes I wonder what's so good about them.

Through the years, we say good-bye to friends, neighborhoods, jobs, relationships, youth, loved ones, and finally, to life itself.

Cowgirl gave me the opportunity to learn how to live through big-time loss.

It happened so suddenly. I saw Cowgirl standing still in the middle of the living room looking down. I offered her a treat, a sip of water, a walk. She just stood there, not moving.

After about ten minutes (it seemed like forever), I lifted all forty-six pounds of her and put her in the car for a quick ride to the vet. My mind and heart were racing. Her behavior was completely unfamiliar.

After many tests and x-rays, the doctor shook his head and said sadly, "It's stomach cancer. We can open her up tomorrow to see if it's operable."

*In the darkest hour, the soul
is replenished and given
strength to continue and endure.*

Heart Warrior Chosa

I felt shocked and panicked. Was he right? Should I get a second opinion? Maybe he had mixed up the x-rays and test results.

When I tried to coax Cowgirl to come with me to think about this at home, she refused. The animal hospital was her least favorite place and now she didn't want to leave! I honored her and left her overnight, partly glad she wouldn't see my pain.

After the exploratory surgery early the next morning, the doctor called. In a very quiet voice he said, "Cowgirl's tumor is the most aggressive type. We can remove it and give her some chemotherapy, but her chances are slim. I'm really sorry. You make the call."

"Go," I said with no hesitation. "Let's not give up. Give it the noblest try you've got in you."

A week after surgery and countless visits with her, I painfully conceded that Cowgirl was fading. She was on morphine now and I could see the spirit was beginning to leave her big brown eyes.

The veterinary staff offered to carry Cowgirl on a blanket to the small field behind the facility so we could have time together outside. Just us.

The sky was the bluest I have ever seen. A few bil-

God gave burdens,
also shoulders.

Yiddish Proverb

lowy, white clouds magnified the contrast and a soft wind blew Cowgirl's flaxen hair.

As I lay on the grass beside her and we looked into each other's eyes, I thanked her for all she had given me over the past eleven years. I don't know how many years she might have given someone else before that.

She looked and listened intently as I reminded her of the joy, love, security, and wisdom she had showered me with. I tearfully told her that if she needed to move on to the next world, I would understand.

Just as I said that, Cowgirl wistfully looked away from me and up toward that beautiful sky. Her eyes followed the clouds ... almost with an expression of longing.

Through my tears, I looked down at the grass between my fingers and into the face of a four-leaf clover. I picked it as a reminder of that bittersweet experience.

The next day, Cowgirl was given increased doses of morphine for the pain. Then I knew the time had come.

I took a deep breath and told the doctor I was

Life is eternal and love is immortal; and death is only a horizon.

Rossiter Raymond

ready to let her go. I had to, for her. But I wanted it to somehow be very special.

My sister Mary Beth offered to be there for Cowgirl and for me. We placed a feather, a silver heart, and her red bandana on her shoulder as she lay quietly on her side.

While the doctor slowly injected the final dose, Mary Beth and I laid our hands on Cowgirl. We cried and cried. We encouraged her spirit to have a smooth trip to heaven. We said a prayer of thanks to God for creating her. We kissed her good-bye. We hugged each other for a long time.

In Cowgirl's memory, Mary Beth and I went back to my place, tearfully toasted her life, and celebrated her with a spaghetti dinner. Cowgirl's favorite, remember?

Through the years, the veterinary staff had fallen in love with Cowgirl, too. In fact the vet's assistant, Kathy Whitsitt, wrote this in a card to her:

Ride 'em Cowgirl,
Taming the clouds,
Lassoing the stars,
Your spirit captured us,
And won our hearts.
We will miss you always.

If we don't grieve…
we can't grow.

CGA

I had never experienced the loss of someone so close. I passionately dreaded it, thinking that it would do me in completely … that I'd never, ever get through it.

Cowgirl taught both Mary Beth and me that death is as sure as life. She gave us the opportunity to experience letting go of a part of the family … someone we dearly cherished.

Exactly eight months to the day of Cowgirl's passing on, I used those lessons with all my might. My precious sister Mary Beth graduated to heaven after a long struggle with breast cancer.

During her last days, my whole family gathered around her … singing, crying, praying, and letting her go. It was terribly hard, but I now knew from experience we would somehow get through it.

Mary Beth's spirit left in peace and love. We left the hospital and the entire family came over to my place. In Mary Beth's honor, we toasted this angelic, colorful, beautiful treasure and enjoyed a pasta dinner. (Sound familiar?)

The next day, we planned a joyous memorial service for her. We celebrated her life, love, her gorgeous spirit, her music and her artwork. No one will ever forget it.

Warm summer sun,
shine kindly here;
blow softly here;
Green sod above,
lie light, lie light-
Goodnight, dear heart,
Goodnight, goodnight.

Mark Twain

As Billy Graham has said,

> *"We need to be reminded that there is nothing morbid about honestly confronting the fact of life's end, and preparing for it so that we may go gracefully and peacefully. The fact is, we cannot truly face life until we have learned to face the fact that it will be taken away from us."*

Sometimes the most painful life experiences are the most profound.

Callie

Part Three:

Healing

*Our dogs live life fully
right up to death. Do we?*

CGA

Our dear pets have become woven into the fabric of our lives. They are an intimate part of us. They are part of the family. They've been loving, fun, faithful and true.

When they die, we may wonder how we will ever smile again. How will our hearts ever mend? It's a crushing blow.

There is hope through healing. Going through a loss is a process. Not an easy one. Everyone walks one's own healing pathway ... and in one's own style.

As you've probably experienced, a loss can bring up many different emotions: sadness, anger, confusion, guilt, fear ... maybe even relief that our loved one is free of pain.

Mourning is important. It's a form of cleansing of the spirit. If we don't grieve, our extreme feelings get pushed away, but they don't go away. They may pop up somewhere down the road and have an affect on us physically and emotionally.

The healing process requires us to go through three stages according to the experts. First is shock, denial, and numbness. Next is fear, anger, depression. Last is understanding, acceptance, and moving on.

*We are healed of a suffering
only by experiencing
it to the fullest.*

Marcel Proust

Yes, it sure takes some doing to get to that moving on part! It doesn't mean that we're over it ... all done. The memories of our beloved pets will always be with us. Again, we must give ourselves all the time we need to get there.

Learning how to grieve is a gift we can use the rest of our lives. Loss is a part of living.

To help your healing, I encourage you to write a letter to a beloved pet you may have lost. Share all your thoughts and feelings. I believe the spirit of our pet receives the message ... and it does our heart good to write it down.

Consider collecting your favorite photos of your pet and putting them in a small booklet along with the letter and special memories. What a nice keepsake you'll have.

Life does go on. It's been almost seven years since Cowgirl's departing. Her memory still visits regularly. It's always pleasant.

Exactly one week after Cowgirl's death, I ran into the veterinarian's assistant at the post office. She was the one who wrote the great poem. We both got teary talking about how we missed Cowgirl, and what a wonderful spirit she had.

Some angels have wings…
some have four paws.

CGA

A few hours later, the phone rang. It was the vet's office saying that several days ago, someone brought in a small dog that had been lost and running down the highway. She kind of reminded them of Cowgirl.

Since no one claimed her, I accepted the invitation to just drop by and see her. Of course ... that was it! We bonded during that short visit and I adopted her.

Callie didn't replace Cowgirl. She filled a new space created out of the blue. Another angel.

There are countless other angels just waiting to share their life, love, and lessons with you ... in time.

Cowgirl, I've always wanted to say...

Dear Cowgirl,

I will miss you forever. And I'll be alright because of you.

Thank you for teaching me how to handle loss with strength, courage, and vulnerability all at once. A meaningful gift.

Thank you for your sweet, faithful love and _all_ your life lessons.

Your red bandana hangs in the hall. Your memory lives in my heart. Ride on Cowgirl.

I will love you always,
Carol Grace

How many other people do you know who might benefit from the ideas and inspiration in *Some Angels Have Four Paws?* Show someone you care. This is a gift to be treasured and appreciated.

Also available from Rock Hill Publishing:

Get Fired-Up Without Burning Out!® Carol Grace Anderson's first book. Here are 180 pages filled with motivating solutions to living a fired-up life.

Get Fired-Up! 10-song CD - A unique collection of upbeat songs to empower you and lift your spirits.

To order by phone call toll-free:
877-446-9364
Order online: www.getfiredup.com